Instant Savings
"3 Saving Strategies No One Talks About"

I0468315

Dr. Ephraim Increase

Instant Savings

Ephraim Economics

ephraimeconomics.com

drephraimincrease.wix.com/ephraimeconomics

Instant Savings by Dr. Ephraim Increase

Copyright © 2016 Ephraim Increase

ISBN-13: 978-1523980468

ISBN-10: 152398046X

First Printing—March 2016

This publication is designed to provide information in regard to the subject matter covered. It is published with the understanding that the author is not engaged in rendering legal counsel or other professional services. If legal advice or other professional advice is required, the services of a professional person should be sought.

Printed in the U.S.A.

Dedication

I dedicate this book to all the individuals that are ready to enjoy the financial rewards of tomorrow by making smart saving decisions TODAY! If you're ready to start saving consistently in order to have the financial future you want and deserve then this book is dedicated you.

Table of Contents

Introduction

Instant Savings, this is what everyone want to manifest in their finances. No matter where you are financially today there is a financial plan for your life. Many time individuals believe that all hope is lost for their finances and they completely give up on seeing a change in their financial situation.

Well it's obvious that you have not completely given up because you have taken the initiative to purchase this book. You will not be disappointed because we will show you a workable plan that will fit any income amount. It doesn't matter if:

- You're a non-professional or professional.
- You know nothing about finances.
- You have never had a budget in your life.

- You think that there is no financial plan for your income.
- You've tried to save and failed many times.

Instant Savings is the book for you and it will show you a workable plan that will be applicable for your financial situation. If you're ready then I am ready to show you how to put money in your savings and change your financial situation **STARTING TODAY!** This book will become your greatest financial companion, so keep it in a safe place where you can go through the strategies on a daily basis using this simple program that will put money into your savings.

1

As Within So Without

"For as he thinketh in his heart, so is he." Proverbs 23:7

Your financial life is literally a reflection of your attitude and understanding about money. Your financial state has arranged itself to bring to you what you believe and to reflect that belief as your financial reality. You are not where you are financially by osmosis or just because. Financially you are where you are because of your thinking and what you have conceived about money matters. Therefore your financial state is an exact reflection of your inner thinking about money. *As within so without.*

Whatever your current financial status is, whether it's zero, twenty dollars, hundreds or thousands in your savings you have manifested that and no more.

Whatever the financial mindset that has the ascendency in your life you have attracted that to your account. Some individuals have a mindset of:

- I am unable to save anything.
- I barely make enough to pay the bills.
- I only live paycheck to paycheck.
- I will struggle financially all the days of my life.
- Maybe poverty is my lot in life.

Always remember that financial success within leads to financial success without. *As within, so without.* Therefore if you want to change your financial situation without, you must look within and change your attitude, mental state and belief about money in order for your outward financial state to change.

Our foundation scripture states, *"For as he thinketh in his heart, so is he." Proverbs 23:7* Literally what this mean in reference to finances is you are where you are financially as a result of what you're thinking financially. Change your thinking financially on the inside and watch what happens financially on the outside. The change begins with you; no one can make this change for you but you. Therefore, your desire to change must be greater than your desire to remain the same. The change that you're looking for financially is not outward but inward.

- It's not a better job making more money.
- It's not winning the lottery *(because without the right thoughts about money you will lose it like so many others have)*.
- It's not a second job to supplement your income.
- It's not a business of your own.
- It's a new attitude!

Honestly, if you want the finances in your life to change, then you must change your mental attitude and belief in life. You must come to the realization that:

1. Money belongs to you.
2. Money is good not bad.
3. You can save money.
4. You have a right to financial success.
5. Saving starts with what you have, not with what you don't have.
6. You must focus on what is not what isn't.
7. If you want the things in your life to change then you must change the things in your life.

If you're ready to take action then we will present to you 3 Savings Strategies that no one talks about. You will have to decide which strategy will best fit you and where you want to start. As you begin to follow these saving strategies you must reject all opposition and all negative thoughts that confront you and try to get you to fall prey to your old way of thinking. You must realize that the word of God says that *"Beloved, I wish above all things that thou mayest prosper and be in health, even as thy soul prospereth."* 3 John 2 The financial prosperity of your life will be a direct reflection of the prosperity of your soul. *As within, so without.*

- Every imagination
- Every negative thought
- Every pessimistic attitude
- Every defeatist financial image
- Every gloomy financial forecast
- Every critical word
- Every ineffective outcome

You must cast it down and remember the word of God says, *"Casting down imaginations, and every high thing that exalteth itself against the knowledge of God, and bringing into captivity every thought to the obedience of Christ; And having a readiness to revenge all disobedience, when your obedience is fulfilled."* 2 Corinthians 10:5-6

If you want something financially that you've never had before, then you must do something financially that you've never done before. Today is the day to begin anew. *As within, so without.* Let's do this!

2
Instant Savings — 3 Saving Strategies That No One Talks About

"The thing that hath been, it is that which shall be; and that which is done is that which shall be done: and there is no new thing under the sun."
Ecclesiastes 1:9

Do you want *Instant Savings*? If you do then you have to realize that you're already in a position to begin saving. You will learn throughout this book that some individuals are in a better position financially to save than others but all are in a position to save, they just don't know it.

Through *Instant Savings*, I will show you how to begin right where you are to begin the process of saving. Let's define these two words of Instant and Savings.

- Instant is defined as: The point of time now. Something happening or coming immediately, without delay right now. What you can do at this time and in this moment.

- Saving is defined as: An amount of money that one has or will save. An amount of something that is not spent or used. An amount of money that you can save especially over a period of time.

Now that we have the definitions of *Instant Savings* we can combine the two to give us a conclusion of our objective for this book. *Instant Savings* is something that you can do right now without delay, an act that you can take immediately financially that you will not spend or use in order to accumulate money over a period of time.

For some of you that act may be mere pennies, for others it may be dollars and still for others you may be able to start at a higher currency for a greater accumulative increase. The fact of the matter is that every person reading this book has the potential to act now without delay for the advancement of their saving portfolio. You may say you don't have anything to start with, I say you do but you just don't know it. I say to you in this instant get your mind off of the big picture and face the immediate picture of where you are right **NOW!**

Remember the first chapter of this book, *As within, so without.* All change begins from within and it progress from there to without. If you're willing to change within and say as I say to you, "You do have something to start with" then the progress and process will begin. Are you ready and willing to begin the process with a spiritual, positive mental attitude? If you are then let me lead you and you just follow and if you do as I say on a daily basis you will accumulate money and change your entire financial perspective and savings portfolio.

Remember "If you want the things in your life to change then you must change the things in your life." *As within, so without.*

The Broke Saver

3

The Broke Person Saving Strategy

"Then he which had received the one talent came and said, Lord, I knew thee that thou art an hard man, reaping where thou hast not sown, and gathered where thou hast now strawed: And I was afraid, and went and hid thy talent in the earth: lo there thou hast that is thine." Matthew 25:24-25

We will begin by stating this strategy first because of the simple fact that it is a strategy that everyone can do. You may want to start with one of the other strategies from the outset but if you're not ready then this strategy will prepare you for future more in-depth strategies that we will cover.

The broke person saving strategy is one that all can truly partake of. I want you to also notice the term I used for this strategy. I did not say the poor person strategy but **the broke person strategy** and the reason is because poor is a state of mind whereas broke is a temporary situation. Even though it has been a long temporary situation for many, that's because to them they are poor within so their poverty reflects without.

This strategy that you will learn here is very simple but it will create great financial dividends if you follow the process. We will use the concept of the widow's mite recorded in the scriptures as the lady that threw in two mites or two cents into the collection plate. So the story goes like this "*And Jesus sat over against the treasury, and beheld how the people cast money into the treasury: and many that were rich cast in much. And there came a certain poor widow, and she threw in two mites, which make a farthing. And he called unto him his disciples, and saith unto them, Verily I say unto you, That this poor widow hath cast more in, than all they which have cast into the treasury: For they did cast in of their abundance; but she of her want did cast in all that she had, even all her living.*" Mark 12:41-44

The Broke Person Saving Strategy will consist of *starting out with 1 cent*. Do you have 1 cent right now, immediately, at this instant that you can begin your process and progress of accumulation or savings?

Before your mind tries to defeat the progress of your new saving strategy with the belief of **"what in the world is 1 cent going to do for me?"** Well, just looking at **1 cent** within itself not much but looking at the end results of 1 cent using the broke person saving strategy that we will use here it will produce for you **$667.95.** Now my question to you is do you at this present time have **$667.95** in your savings account? Did you save **$667.95** last year using any type of saving plan to help you get ahead? Last question, did you save this much in the last 3 years with any type of savings plan or strategy? If you can answer yes to these questions then this plan is not for you we have other saving strategies that will be more conducive for you.

However, we will go over this strategy for those whom their answer would be no to these questions.

The Broke Person Strategy is simple and we will use every day to accomplish the goal of having a savings of **$667.95** within a 1 year period. There are 365 days in the year and each and every day your first objective of the day is to put aside 1 cent accumulative over the next 365 days. Here's how it will look and the simplicity of the strategy:

1. **Day 1 = 1 cent**
2. **Day 2 = 2 cents**
3. **Day 3 = 3 cents**
4. **Day 4 = 4 cents**
5. **Day 5 = 5 cents**
6. **Day 6 = 6 cents**
7. **Day 7 = 7 cents**

So looking at just 1 week of doing this how much would you have saved in 1 week? Some people would think, well 7 cents. Not exactly, you have actually saved **28 cents** in 7 days. If you add up all that you have put in your savings jar for 7 days it will add up to **28 cents.** You may think that this is a slow process. Yes and no, what is happening is the concept and strategy is getting you in the **HABIT** of saving daily and any habit done for a minimum of 21 days will help equip you to adapt to a new pattern or change in your life. If you continue this pattern for 66 days then the new behavior will become an automatic habit and pattern in your life.

The way the saving strategy works is you can do the daily amount as stated above on the example or you can do any of the amounts on a daily basis. You only have to make sure that every amount is done in the example within 365 days. For example you can do day 1 and put in 1 cent and do day 25 for 25 cents the next day and do day 3 for 3 cents the third day etc... You can mix it up or do according to the daily amount in sequence. The key to the whole strategy is that every single amount must be covered within the 365 day period and when it is then you will have accumulated a total of **$667.95** at the end of 1 year or 365 days. If you will follow the pattern in 1 year's time you will have more money in savings than you have had in a long time. The strategy is simple and anyone can do it. Once you have put that amount in then you can simply scratch through that amount in the book as completed on that day. Here is how much should be done daily or all that needs to be covered in 365 days.

The Broke Person Saving Strategy

Day 1 = 1 cents
Day 2 = 2 cents
Day 3 = 3 cents
Day 4 = 4 cents
Day 5 = 5 cents
Day 6 = 6 cents
Day 7 = 7 cents
Day 8 = 8 cents
Day 9 = 9 cents
Day 10 = 10 cents
Day 11 = 11 cents

Instant Savings

Day 12 = 12 cents
Day 13 = 13 cents
Day 14 = 14 cents
Day 15 = 15 cents
Day 16 = 16 cents
Day 17 = 17 cents
Day 18 = 18 cents
Day 19 = 19 cents
Day 20 = 20 cents
Day 21 = 21 cents
Day 22 = 22 cents
Day 23 = 23 cents
Day 24 = 24 cents
Day 25 = 25 cents
Day 26 = 26 cents
Day 27 = 27 cents
Day 28 = 28 cents
Day 29 = 29 cents
Day 30 = 30 cents
Day 31 = 31 cents
Day 32 = 32 cents
Day 33 = 33 cents
Day 34 = 34 cents
Day 35 = 35 cents
Day 36 = 36 cents
Day 37 = 37 cents
Day 38 = 38 cents
Day 39 = 39 cents
Day 40 = 40 cents
Day 41 = 41 cents
Day 42 = 42 cents

Day 43 = 43 cents
Day 44 = 44 cents
Day 45 = 45 cents
Day 46 = 46 cents
Day 47 = 47 cents
Day 48 = 48 cents
Day 49 = 49 cents
Day 50 = 50 cents
Day 51 = 51 cents
Day 52 = 52 cents
Day 53 = 53 cents
Day 54 = 54 cents
Day 55 = 55 cents
Day 56 = 56 cents
Day 57 = 57 cents
Day 58 = 58 cents
Day 59 = 59 cents
Day 60 = 60 cents
Day 61 = 61 cents
Day 62 = 62 cents
Day 63 = 63 cents
Day 64 = 64 cents
Day 65 = 65 cents
Day 66 = 66 cents
Day 67 = 67 cents
Day 68 = 68 cents
Day 69 = 69 cents
Day 70 = 70 cents
Day 71 = 71 cents
Day 72 = 72 cents
Day 73 = 73 cents

Day 74 = 74 cents
Day 75 = 75 cents
Day 76 = 76 cents
Day 77 = 77 cents
Day 78 = 78 cents
Day 79 = 79 cents
Day 80 = 80 cents
Day 81 = 81 cents
Day 82 = 82 cents
Day 83 = 83 cents
Day 84 = 84 cents
Day 85 = 85 cents
Day 86 = 86 cents
Day 87 = 87 cents
Day 88 = 88 cents
Day 89 = 89 cents
Day 90 = 90 cents
Day 91 = 91 cents
Day 92 = 92 cents
Day 93 = 93 cents
Day 94 = 94 cents
Day 95 = 95 cents
Day 96 = 96 cents
Day 97 = 97 cents
Day 98 = 98 cents
Day 99 = 99 cents
Day 100 = 1 dollar
Day 101 = 1dollar & 1 cent
Day 102 = 1 dollar & 2 cents
Day 103 = 1 dollar & 3 cents
Day 104 = 1 dollar & 4 cents

Instant Savings

Day 105 = 1 dollar & 5 cents
Day 106 = 1 dollar & 6 cents
Day 107 = 1 dollar & 7 cents
Day 108 = 1 dollar & 8 cents
Day 109 = 1 dollar & 9 cents
Day 110 = 1 dollar & 10 cents
Day 111 = 1 dollar & 11 cents
Day 112 = 1 dollar & 12 cents
Day 113 = 1 dollar & 13 cents
Day 114 = 1 dollar & 14 cents
Day 115 = 1 dollar & 15 cents
Day 116 = 1 dollar & 16 cents
Day 117 = 1 dollar & 17 cents
Day 118 = 1 dollar & 18 cents
Day 119 = 1 dollar & 19 cents
Day 120 = 1 dollar & 20 cents
Day 121 = 1 dollar & 21 cents
Day 122 = 1 dollar & 22 cents
Day 123 = 1 dollar & 23 cents
Day 124 = 1 dollar & 24 cents
Day 125 = 1 dollar & 25 cents
Day 126 = 1 dollar & 26 cents
Day 127 = 1 dollar & 27 cents
Day 128 = 1 dollar & 28 cents
Day 129 = 1 dollar & 29 cents
Day 130 = 1 dollar & 30 cents
Day 131 = 1 dollar & 31 cent
Day 132 = 1 dollar & 32 cents
Day 133 = 1 dollar & 33 cents
Day 134 = 1 dollar & 34 cents
Day 135 = 1 dollar & 35 cents

Instant Savings

Day 136 = 1 dollar & 36 cents
Day 137 = 1 dollar & 37 cents
Day 138 = 1 dollar & 38 cents
Day 139 = 1 dollar & 39 cents
Day 140 = 1 dollar & 40 cents
Day 141 = 1 dollar & 41 cents
Day 142 = 1 dollar & 42 cents
Day 143 = 1 dollar & 43 cents
Day 144 = 1 dollar & 44 cents
Day 145 = 1 dollar & 45 cents
Day 146 = 1 dollar & 46 cents
Day 147 = 1 dollar & 47 cents
Day 148 = 1 dollar & 48 cents
Day 149 = 1 dollar & 49 cents
Day 150 = 1 dollar & 50 cents
Day 151 = 1 dollar & 51 cents
Day 152 = 1 dollar & 52 cents
Day 153 = 1 dollar & 53 cents
Day 154 = 1 dollar & 54 cents
Day 155 = 1 dollar & 55 cents
Day 156 = 1 dollar & 56 cents
Day 157 = 1 dollar & 57 cents
Day 158 = 1 dollar & 58 cents
Day 159 = 1 dollar & 59 cents
Day 160 = 1 dollar & 60 cents
Day 161 = 1 dollar & 61 cents
Day 162 = 1 dollar & 62 cents
Day 163 = 1 dollar & 63 cents
Day 164 = 1 dollar & 64 cents
Day 165 = 1 dollar & 65 cents
Day 166 = 1 dollar & 66 cents

Day 167 = 1 dollar & 67 cents
Day 168 = 1 dollar & 68 cents
Day 169 = 1 dollar & 69 cents
Day 170 = 1 dollar & 70 cents
Day 171 = 1 dollar & 71 cents
Day 172 = 1 dollar & 72 cents
Day 173 = 1 dollar & 73 cents
Day 174 = 1 dollar & 74 cents
Day 175 = 1 dollar & 75 cents
Day 176 = 1 dollar & 76 cents
Day 177 = 1 dollar & 77 cents
Day 178 = 1 dollar & 78 cents
Day 179 = 1 dollar & 79 cents
Day 180 = 1 dollar & 80 cents
Day 181 = 1 dollar & 81 cents
Day 182 = 1 dollar & 82 cents
Day 183 = 1 dollar & 83 cents
Day 184 = 1 dollar & 84 cents
Day 185 = 1 dollar & 85 cents
Day 186 = 1 dollar & 86 cents
Day 187 = 1 dollar & 87 cents
Day 188 = 1 dollar & 88 cents
Day 189 = 1 dollar & 89 cents
Day 190 = 1 dollar & 90 cents
Day 191 = 1 dollar & 91 cent
Day 192 = 1 dollar & 92 cents
Day 193 = 1 dollar & 93 cents
Day 194 = 1 dollar & 94 cents
Day 195 = 1 dollar & 95 cents
Day 196 = 1 dollar & 96 cents
Day 197 = 1 dollar & 97 cents

Day 198 = 1 dollar & 98 cents
Day 199 = 1 dollar & 99 cents
Day 200 = 2 dollars & 00 cents
Day 201 = 2 dollars & 1 cent
Day 202 = 2 dollars & 2 cents
Day 203 = 2 dollars & 3 cents
Day 204 = 2 dollars & 4 cents
Day 205 = 2 dollars & 5 cents
Day 206 = 2 dollars & 6 cents
Day 207 = 2 dollars & 7 cents
Day 208 = 2 dollars & 8 cents
Day 209 = 2 dollars & 9 cents
Day 210 = 2 dollars & 10 cents
Day 211 = 2 dollars & 11 cents
Day 212 = 2 dollars & 12 cents
Day 213 = 2 dollars & 13 cents
Day 214 = 2 dollars & 14 cents
Day 215 = 2 dollars & 15 cents
Day 216 = 2 dollars & 16 cents
Day 217 = 2 dollars & 17 cents
Day 218 = 2 dollars & 18 cents
Day 219 = 2 dollars & 19 cents
Day 220 = 2 dollars & 00 cents
Day 221 = 2 dollars & 21 cents
Day 222 = 2 dollars & 22 cents
Day 223 = 2 dollars & 23 cents
Day 224 = 2 dollars & 24 cents
Day 225 = 2 dollars & 25 cents
Day 226 = 2 dollars & 26 cents
Day 227 = 2 dollars & 27 cents
Day 228 = 2 dollars & 28 cents

Day 229 = 2 dollars & 29 cents
Day 230 = 2 dollars & 30 cents
Day 231 = 2 dollars & 31 cents
Day 232 = 2 dollars & 32 cents
Day 233 = 2 dollars & 33 cents
Day 234 = 2 dollars & 34 cents
Day 235 = 2 dollars & 35 cents
Day 236 = 2 dollars & 36 cents
Day 237 = 2 dollars & 37 cents
Day 238 = 2 dollars & 38 cents
Day 239 = 2 dollars & 39 cents
Day 240 = 2 dollars & 40 cents
Day 241 = 2 dollars & 41 cents
Day 242 = 2 dollars & 42 cents
Day 243 = 2 dollars & 43 cents
Day 244 = 2 dollars & 44 cents
Day 245 = 2 dollars & 45 cents
Day 246 = 2 dollars & 46 cents
Day 247 = 2 dollars & 47 cents
Day 248 = 2 dollars & 48 cents
Day 249 = 2 dollars & 49 cents
Day 250 = 2 dollars & 50 cents
Day 251 = 2 dollars & 51 cents
Day 252 = 2 dollars & 52 cents
Day 253 = 2 dollars & 53 cents
Day 254 = 2 dollars & 54 cents
Day 255 = 2 dollars & 55 cents
Day 256 = 2 dollars & 56 cents
Day 257 = 2 dollars & 57 cents
Day 258 = 2 dollars & 58 cents
Day 259 = 2 dollars & 59 cents

Day 260 = 2 dollars & 60 cents
Day 261 = 2 dollars & 61 cents
Day 262 = 2 dollars & 62 cents
Day 263 = 2 dollars & 63 cents
Day 264 = 2 dollars & 64 cents
Day 265 = 2 dollars & 65 cents
Day 266 = 2 dollars & 66 cents
Day 267 = 2 dollars & 67 cents
Day 268 = 2 dollars & 68 cents
Day 269 = 2 dollars & 69 cents
Day 270 = 2 dollars & 70 cents
Day 271 = 2 dollars & 71 cents
Day 272 = 2 dollars & 72 cents
Day 273 = 2 dollars & 73 cents
Day 274 = 2 dollars & 74 cents
Day 275 = 2 dollars & 75 cents
Day 276 = 2 dollars & 76 cents
Day 277 = 2 dollars & 77 cents
Day 278 = 2 dollars & 78 cents
Day 279 = 2 dollars & 79 cents
Day 280 = 2 dollars & 80 cents
Day 281 = 2 dollars & 81 cents
Day 282 = 2 dollars & 82 cents
Day 283 = 2 dollars & 83 cents
Day 284 = 2 dollars & 84 cents
Day 285 = 2 dollars & 85 cents
Day 286 = 2 dollars & 86 cents
Day 287 = 2 dollars & 87 cents
Day 288 = 2 dollars & 88 cents
Day 289 = 2 dollars & 89 cents
Day 290 = 2 dollars & 90 cents

Instant Savings

Day 291 = 2 dollars & 91 cents
Day 292 = 2 dollars & 92 cents
Day 293 = 2 dollars & 93 cents
Day 294 = 2 dollars & 94 cents
Day 295 = 2 dollars & 95 cents
Day 296 = 2 dollars & 96 cents
Day 297 = 2 dollars & 97 cents
Day 298 = 2 dollars & 98 cents
Day 299 = 2 dollars & 99 cents
Day 300 = 3 dollars & 00 cents
Day 301 = 3 dollars & 1 cents
Day 302 = 3 dollars & 2 cents
Day 303 = 3 dollars & 3 cents
Day 304 = 3 dollars & 4 cents
Day 305 = 3 dollars & 5 cents
Day 306 = 3 dollars & 6 cents
Day 307 = 3 dollars & 7 cents
Day 308 = 3 dollars & 8 cents
Day 309 = 3 dollars & 9 cents
Day 310 = 3 dollars & 10 cents
Day 311 = 3 dollars & 11 cents
Day 312 = 3 dollars & 12 cents
Day 313 = 3 dollars & 13 cents
Day 314 = 3 dollars & 14 cents
Day 315 = 3 dollars & 15 cents
Day 316 = 3 dollars & 16 cents
Day 317 = 3 dollars & 17 cents
Day 318 = 3 dollars & 18 cents
Day 319 = 3 dollars & 19 cents
Day 320 = 3 dollars & 20 cents
Day 321 = 3 dollars & 21 cents

Instant Savings

Day 322 = 3 dollars & 22 cents
Day 323 = 3 dollars & 23 cents
Day 324 = 3 dollars & 24 cents
Day 325 = 3 dollars & 25 cents
Day 326 = 3 dollars & 26 cents
Day 327 = 3 dollars & 27 cents
Day 328 = 3 dollars & 28 cents
Day 329 = 3 dollars & 29 cents
Day 330 = 3 dollars & 30 cents
Day 331 = 3 dollars & 31 cents
Day 332 = 3 dollars & 32 cents
Day 333 = 3 dollars & 33 cents
Day 334 = 3 dollars & 34 cents
Day 335 = 3 dollars & 35 cents
Day 336 = 3 dollars & 36 cents
Day 337 = 3 dollars & 37 cents
Day 338 = 3 dollars & 38 cents
Day 339 = 3 dollars & 39 cents
Day 340 = 3 dollars & 40 cents
Day 341 = 3 dollars & 41 cents
Day 342 = 3 dollars & 42 cents
Day 343 = 3 dollars & 43 cents
Day 344 = 3 dollars & 44 cents
Day 345 = 3 dollars & 45 cents
Day 346 = 3 dollars & 46 cents
Day 347 = 3 dollars & 47 cents
Day 348 = 3 dollars & 48 cents
Day 349 = 3 dollars & 49 cents
Day 350 = 3 dollars & 50 cents
Day 351 = 3 dollars & 51 cents
Day 352 = 3 dollars & 52 cents

Day 353 = 3 dollars & 53 cents
Day 354 = 3 dollars & 54 cents
Day 355 = 3 dollars & 55 cents
Day 356 = 3 dollars & 56 cents
Day 357 = 3 dollars & 57 cents
Day 358 = 3 dollars & 58 cents
Day 359 = 3 dollars & 59 cents
Day 360 = 3 dollars & 60 cents
Day 361 = 3 dollars & 61 cents
Day 362 = 3 dollars & 62 cents
Day 363 = 3 dollars & 63 cents
Day 364 = 3 dollars & 64 cents
Day 365 = 3 dollars & 65 cents

Once every day is marked off within 365 days you have completed your saving strategy and now have a whopping **$667.95.** Remember you don't have to go in sequence day by day if you don't desire to. You can skip around but something must be put in your jar on a daily basis. If you only have **5 pennies** to your name then use this for day 5 and mark through that day. Whereas another day you may have **$1.50** you want to put in so you will use that for day 150 and so on and so forth. At the end of your journey you will have accumulated your financial goal of acquiring **$667.95** for your first year goal.

However, if you like you can also use this strategy alone with the other strategies that we will go over simply to add to your bottom line more expedient. We want to make this transaction into savings as flawless and proficient as possible for you. What I have done in my saving strategy that has really helped expedite and caused my saving to be creative and fun is to save my money in a *"Digital Counting Coin Bank Savings Jar."* This jar automatically totals up my savings for me and I don't have to get into the habit of having to count what I'm saving because it does it for me automatically. You can see and order one if you like, which I highly recommend by going to my website at:

www.ephraimeconomics.com or

www.drephraimincrease.wix.com/ephraimecon omics#!saving-strategies/c1pna

The Conservative Saver

4

The Conservative Person
Saving Strategy

"Then he which had received the five talents went and traded with the same, and made them other five talents. And so he that had received five talents came and brought other five talents, saying, Lord, thou deliveredst unto me five talents: behold, I have gained beside them five talents more " Matthew 25:16, 20

The next saving strategy that we will observe is **the Conservative Person Saving Strategy**. This is a saving strategy that is a little more challenging than the broke person saving strategy, that's why I opted to make it the second strategy. However, if you have successfully done the first strategy then your habit of saving is already on point. Nevertheless, if you're starting out with **the Conservative Person Saving Strategy** then it will yield a greater financial reward.

This strategy is based on a weekly saving instead of a daily strategy saving.

We will call this the **"52 Week Saving Strategy"** where we will ask you to save a certain amount each week. Well, this saving strategy has equipped many individuals to save when they were never able to save before. Saving a certain amount weekly equips you to build a savings in a realistic way, even when things are slow.

The key to this **52 week saving strategy** is to save a certain amount each week starting with a small amount of just **$1.** When this is done consistently it will yield you **$1,378.00** at the end of the 52 week period. Here's how it will look and the simplicity of the strategy:

1. Week 1 = $1 saved
2. Week 2 = $2 saved
3. Week 3 = $3 saved
4. Week 4 = $4 saved
5. Week 5 = $5 saved
6. Week 6 = $6 saved
7. Week 7 = $7 saved

So looking at just 7 weeks of doing this how much would you have saved in 7 weeks? If you add it all up you would have put in your savings jar for 7 weeks a total amount of **28 dollars**. Would you believe that somebody somewhere don't even have **$28** in a savings? Well, even if this may be you your outward financial portfolio is getting ready to change because the change begins from within. As you change your attitude and mindset about saving it will soon begin to reflect in your outward circumstances. *As within, so without.*

Well, just looking at starting with 1 dollar may not seem like much but looking at the end results of 1 dollar using **the conservative person strategy** that we will use here it will produce for you **$1,378.00.** Now my question to you is do you at this present time have **$1,378.00** in your savings account? Did you save **$1,378.00** last year using any type of savings plan to help you get ahead? Last question, did you save this much in the last 3 years with any type of savings plan or strategy? If you can answer yes to these questions then this plan is not for you we have one more saving strategy that will be more strategic for you.

However, we will go over this strategy for those whom their answer would be no to these questions. **The Conservative Person Strategy** is simple and we will use weekly accomplishments to achieve the goal of having a savings of **$1,378.00** within a 1 year period.

The way the saving strategy works is you can do the weekly amount as stated above on the example or you can do any of the amounts on a weekly basis. You only have to make sure that every amount is done in the example within 52 weeks. For example you can do week 1 and put in **1 dollar** and week 25 for **25 dollars** the next week and do week 3 for **3 dollars** the third week etc... You can mix it up or do according to the weekly amount in sequence. The key is that every single amount must be done in 52 weeks.

When it is done you will have accumulated a total of **$1,378.00** at the end of 1 year or 52 weeks. If you will follow the pattern in 1 year's time you will have more money in savings than you have had in a long time. The strategy is simple and anyone can do it. Once you have put that amount in then you can simply scratch through that amount in the book as completed on that week. Here is how much should be done weekly or all that needs to be covered in 365 days or 52 weeks.

The Conservative Person Saving Strategy

Week 1 = 1 dollar
Week 2 = 2 dollars
Week 3 = 3 dollars
Week 4 = 4 dollars
Week 5 = 5 dollars
Week 6 = 6 dollars
Week 7 = 7 dollars
Week 8 = 8 dollars
Week 9 = 9 dollars
Week 10 = 10 dollars
Week 11 = 11 dollars

Instant Savings

Week 12 = 12 dollars
Week 13 = 13 dollars
Week 14 = 14 dollars
Week 15 = 15 dollars
Week 16 = 16 dollars
Week 17 = 17 dollars
Week 18 = 18 dollars
Week 19 = 19 dollars
Week 20 = 20 dollars
Week 21 = 21 dollars
Week 22 = 22 dollars
Week 23 = 23 dollars
Week 24 = 24 dollars
Week 25 = 25 dollars
Week 26 = 26 dollars
Week 27 = 27 dollars
Week 28 = 28 dollars
Week 29 = 29 dollars
Week 30 = 30 dollars
Week 31 = 31 dollars
Week 32 = 32 dollars
Week 33 = 33 dollars
Week 34 = 34 dollars
Week 35 = 35 dollars
Week 36 = 36 dollars
Week 37 = 37 dollars
Week 38 = 38 dollars
Week 39 = 39 dollars
Week 40 = 40 dollars
Week 41 = 41 dollars
Week 42 = 42 dollars

Week 43 = 43 dollars
Week 44 = 44 dollars
Week 45 = 45 dollars
Week 46 = 46 dollars
Week 47 = 47 dollars
Week 48 = 48 dollars
Week 49 = 49 dollars
Week 50 = 50 dollars
Week 51 = 51 dollars
Week 52 = 52 dollars

Once every week is marked off within 52 weeks you have completed your saving strategy and now have a whopping **$1,378.00.** Remember you don't have to go in sequence week by week if you don't desire to. You can skip around but something must be put in your jar on a weekly basis. If you have **5 dollar** the second week then use this for week 5 and mark through that week. Whereas another week you may have **$50** you want to put in so you will use that for week 50 and so on and so forth. At the end of your journey you will have accumulated your financial goal of acquiring **$1,380.00** for your first year in your saving strategy.

Your goal of course is to put something in every week to move you forward to achievement. The amount will depend on what you can do that week whether it's more, less or exact, and then mark through in this book that amount as accomplished and done in your 52 week journey. And at the end of your journey, like the man with the 5 talents heard for his good and faithful work *"His lord said unto him, Well done, thou good and faithful servant: thou hast been faithful over a few things, I will make thee ruler over many things: enter thou into the joy of thy lord." Matthew 25:21*

If God can trust you being a **conservative saver** then he will bless and grace you to go on **to bigger and better savings.** He will bless you to become an **Aggressive Saver.** For *"He that is faithful in that which is least is faithful also in much: and he that is unjust in the least is unjust in much." Luke 16:10*

The Aggressive Saver

5

The Aggressive Person Saving Strategy

"He becometh poor that dealeth with a slack hand: but the hand of the diligent maketh rich." Proverbs 10:4

This is the final saving strategy that we will observe and it's called **the Aggressive Person Saving Strategy.** This strategy will put money in your account in a major way. This strategy is not for the faint hearted but for those who are ready to pursue their financial aim forcefully.

An **aggressive saver** is one who goes into an attack mode and that's unafraid to confront their finances. An aggressor is:

- Hostile
- Belligerent
- Antagonistic
- Assertive
- Pushy
- Forceful

- Vigorous
- Energetic
- Dynamic

This strategy is also based on a 52 week saving strategy. However, the saving is more forceful and assertive than the **$1 conservative saver.** This saving strategy will help you to amass **$6890.00** in a 52 week period.

The key to this 52 week saving strategy is to save a certain amount each week **starting with an aggressive amount of $5.** When this is done consistently it will yield you **$6,890.00** at the end of the 52 week period. Here's how it will look and the simplicity of the strategy:

1. **Week 1 = $5 saved**
2. **Week 2 = $10 saved**
3. **Week 3 = $15 saved**
4. **Week 4 = $20 saved**
5. **Week 5 = $25 saved**
6. **Week 6 = $30 saved**
7. **Week 7 = $35 saved**

So looking at just 7 week of doing this how much would you have saved in 7 weeks? If you add up all that you have put in your savings jar for 7 weeks it will add up to **$140.00.** Would you believe that somebody somewhere don't even have **$140** in a savings? Some individuals have worked all their life and can't put their hands on **$140** instantly. Well, if you're ready for an outward dynamic financial manifestation **the aggressive saver** is your outlet. Your outward financial portfolio is getting ready to change because you are now the **"Aggressive Saver"** and your vigorous mental state within concerning saving will miraculously make you more profitable than you've ever been. *As within, so without.*

This is a proven and remarkable strategy that will revolutionize your savings portfolio. Have you been able to save **$6,890.00** within the last 5 years? How about the last 10 years? How about the last 20 years? Well I will reveal to you how to do this in 52 weeks or within 1 year. Your savings will skyrocket as you become an **aggressive saver**. What has taken some 10, 20, 30 years or more to do, you will accomplish within 52 weeks.

The Aggressive Person Saving Strategy is simple and we will use weekly accomplishments to achieve the goal of having a savings of **$6,890.00** within a 52 week period.

The way the saving strategy works is you can do the weekly amount as stated above on the example or you can do any of the amounts on a weekly basis. You only have to make sure that every amount is covered and done within 52 weeks. For example you can do week 1 and put in **$5** and week 10 the second week and put in **$50** and week 3 put in **$15** for the third week etc... You can mix it up or do according to the weekly amount in sequence. The key is that every single amount must be done in 52 weeks.

When it is then you will have accumulated a total of **$6,890** at the end of

1 year or 52 weeks. If you will follow the pattern, in 1 year's time your savings account would have exploded. And you will have created your very own fortune, to you this will be like hitting the jackpot and you did it by following a proven method.

The strategy is simple and anyone can do it. Once you have put that amount in then you can simply scratch through that amount as completed on that week. Here is how much should be done weekly or all that needs to be covered in 52 weeks.

The Aggressive Person Saving Strategy

Week 1 = 5 dollars
Week 2 = 10 dollars
Week 3 = 15 dollars
Week 4 = 20 dollars
Week 5 = 25 dollars
Week 6 = 30 dollars
Week 7 = 35 dollars
Week 8 = 40 dollars
Week 9 = 45 dollars
Week 10 = 50 dollars
Week 11 = 55 dollars

Instant Savings

Week 12 = 60 dollars
Week 13 = 65 dollars
Week 14 = 70 dollars
Week 15 = 75 dollars
Week 16 = 80 dollars
Week 17 = 85 dollars
Week 18 = 90 dollars
Week 19 = 95 dollars
Week 20 = 100 dollars
Week 21 = 105 dollars
Week 22 = 110 dollars
Week 23 = 115 dollars
Week 24 = 120 dollars
Week 25 = 125 dollars
Week 26 = 130 dollars
Week 27 = 135 dollars
Week 28 = 140 dollars
Week 29 = 145 dollars
Week 30 = 150 dollars
Week 31 = 155 dollars
Week 32 = 160 dollars
Week 33 = 165 dollars
Week 34 = 170 dollars
Week 35 = 175 dollars
Week 36 = 180 dollars
Week 37 = 185 dollars
Week 38 = 190 dollars
Week 39 = 195 dollars
Week 40 = 200 dollars
Week 41 = 205 dollars
Week 42 = 210 dollars

Week 43 = 215 dollars
Week 44 = 222 dollars
Week 45 = 225 dollars
Week 46 = 230 dollars
Week 47 = 235 dollars
Week 48 = 240 dollars
Week 49 = 245 dollars
Week 50 = 250 dollars
Week 51 = 255 dollars
Week 52 = 260 dollars

Once every week is marked off within 52 weeks you have completed your saving strategy and now have a whopping **$6,890.00**. Remember you don't have to go in sequence week by week if you don't desire to. You can skip around but something must be put in on a weekly basis. If you have **$25** the second week then use this for week 5 and mark through that week. Whereas another week you may have **$250** you want to put in so you will use that for week 50 and so on and so forth. At the end of your journey you will have accumulated your financial goal of acquiring **$6,890.00** for your first year in your saving strategy.

Your goal is to put something in every week to move you forward to achievement. The amount will depend on what you can do that week whether it's more, less or exact, and then mark through in this book that amount as accomplished and done in your 52 week journey. And at the end of your journey, because of your diligence in saving you will be richer than you've ever been.

If God can trust you to be an **aggressive saver** then he will bless and grace you to go on to bigger and better savings and investments. For *"He that is faithful in that which is least is faithful also in much." Luke 16:10a*

Your Savings Portfolio

6

Your Savings Portfolio

"Go to the ant, thou sluggard; consider her ways, and be wise: Which having no guide, overseer, or ruler, Provideth her meat in the summer, and gathereth her food in the harvest." Proverbs 6:6-8

Your savings portfolio can be as big as you desire it to be, but the key is you must get started. If you will get started these strategies are designed to equip you to escape debt and start saving money.

It's not a second job that you need you just need to become focused on saving using one or more of these strategies. You don't need to stress any longer over finances because if you start and continue either of these strategies they will put money in your savings. Here are the 3 strategies again with each saving amount.

1. *The Broke Person Saving Strategy will bank you $667.95.*

2. *The Conservative Person Saving Strategy will bank you $1,378.00.*

3. *The Aggressive Person Saving Strategy will bank you $6,890.00.*

With these 3 saving strategies available gone are the days where you will make excuses that you don't have anything to save. Everyone, can save some money starting with one of these strategies. Your saving portfolio can abound with financial blessings if you will just believe it can and get started right now.

If you are reading this book and have never been able to save, you may say to yourself, "I have no idea what I'm doing", I say to you just follow the strategy. Every day you don't get started you are losing money, because you are a day behind in the strategy. I have made this so simple and easy that you cannot honestly tell me that you can't even begin with strategy #1. You can't tell me that you don't have the money to get started with your savings portfolio. If you say you don't it's your own laziness and negative attitude that has kept you and will continue to keep you failing financially. Strategy #1 tells you to begin on day one with just 1 cent. Surely you have 1 cent just lying around somewhere in your house, this is enough to begin your saving portfolio with day 1. Let's reiterate the first week with strategy #1.

1. **Day 1 = 1 cent**
2. **Day 2 = 2 cents**
3. **Day 3 = 3 cents**
4. **Day 4 = 4 cents**
5. **Day 5 = 5 cents**
6. **Day 6 = 6 cents**
7. **Day 7 = 7 cents**

One big hindrance to saving for many was the amount of money required to get started. Not anymore, because the strategies we've included here is manageable even for a broke person. So even if you are broke with no great amount to get started with or just a little to start with, it's now easier than ever to start saving and seeing your money grow into hundreds and thousands of dollars.

It's time to let your money (even if it's only change) begin to work for you. Making money work for you is no longer a luxury of the rich, with these 3 amazing money saving strategies you will now be equipped to manage your money starting today.

Every day that you wait is another day that you have forfeited money from going in your saving portfolio. Wouldn't you rather have money going in your portfolio than just continually putting money in the hands of your creditors, then you're going to have to do something different. Remember, if you want the things in your life to change then you're going to have to change the things in your life.

No more excuses, now is the time and today is the day to get started. Go now and get that **1 penny** to begin the process

for the **"Broke Person Saving Strategy."**
Or go now and get that **1 dollar** to begin
the process for the **"Conservative Person
Saving Strategy."** Or go now and get that
5 dollars to begin the process for the
"Aggressive Person Saving Strategy."

You can do it, now is the time and
you're the person. You now have in your
possession **"The 3 Saving Strategies No
One Talks About."** You have the secret
to:

- Financial increase
- Financial prosperity
- Financial abundance
- Financial riches
- Financial wealth

You have the inside information that no
one wants to tell you and it will produce
for you remarkable results. I urge you not
to seek for riches in the distance but
realize that these 3 strategies are truly the
fortune that you seek. Embrace them and

allow them to explode and skyrocket you to a financial plateau that you have never had the savings freedom to know before. You are privileged to have this information and it can and will produce astounding results and secure for you a stable and sure financial future. The word of God says, *"Wealth and Riches shall be in his house." Psalms 112:3a* God is ready to bless you, now my question is are you ready to be blessed?

Ephraim Economics Special Notes

1. *If you get paid every two weeks or bi-monthly then you will need to take out the amount of savings for two weeks at a time.*

Ex. The Broker saver will need to take out the amount for 14 days. Each pay period you will need to take out the amounts for 14 days.

Day 1 = 1 cents
Day 2 = 2 cents
Day 3 = 3 cents
Day 4 = 4 cents
Day 5 = 5 cents
Day 6 = 6 cents
Day 7 = 7 cents
Day 8 = 8 cents
Day 9 = 9 cents
Day 10 = 10 cents
Day 11 = 11 cents
Day 12 = 12 cents
Day 13 = 13 cents
Day 14 = 14 cents

The amount you will take out for your first 14 days will be $1.05. The amount you will take out for day 15 through day

28 will be $3.01. Etc…

2. *As a Conservative saver getting paid every two weeks you will need to take out your amount every 2 weeks at your pay period.*

> Week 1 = 1 dollar
> Week 2 = 2 dollars

The amount you will take out for your first 2 weeks will be $3.00. The amount you will take out the following pay period for weeks 3 through 4 will be $7.00. Etc…

> Week 3 = 3 dollars
> Week 4 = 4 dollars

3. *As an Aggressive saver getting paid every two weeks you will need to take out your amount every 2 weeks at your pay period.*

> Week 1 = 5 dollar
> Week 2 = 10 dollars

The amount you will take out for your first 2 weeks will be $15.00. The amount you will take out the following pay period for weeks 3 through 4 will be $35.00. Etc...

> Week 3 = $15 dollars
> Week 4 = $20 dollars

4. It is very important that you keep the book visible where you can see it on a daily basis, until your saving becomes a habit. Seeing the book will be a reminder of your daily or weekly deposits.

5. It is best to save your money in a *"Digital Counting Coin Bank Saving Jar"* to begin with. When the jar is full and has about $100 or $200 in it you can then open up an *"Interest Bearing Savings Account"* to deposit that amount.

6. Also, if you want to put a date next

to the amount you are depositing daily or weekly in your jar you can do so by writing in the book.

7. Make a decision about which strategy you will begin with or whether you want to do a combination of strategies. You can do the *"Broke Person Saving Strategy"* and the *"Conservative Person Saving Strategy"* at the same time. Or you can do the *"Broke Person Saving Strategy"* and the *"Aggressive Person Saving Strategy"* at the same time. Whatever is convenient for you?

8. Lastly, following these strategies allows you to do something that most people never do, which is having a set goal for financial attainment. Having a goal is the difference between financial success and financial failure. Each strategy

gives you a financial goal to work towards and because of this you will succeed financially.

9. In closing I would also encourage you to become a member of the *"Ephraim Economics Membership Club"* for those that are truly serious about changing their financial situation. You will have access to daily or weekly information and importation that others will not have access to. Check us out about membership at: www.ephraimeconomics.com or www.drephraimincrease.wix.com/ephraimeconomics

10. Family & Friends Information. If you have family members or friends that are struggling financially, why don't you get together with them and begin a *"Ephraim Economics Outreach Group"* and use this book for a focus group

to show them how to begin the process and progress of saving money? Even if you start with 2 or 3 serious minded people that are tired of their financial situation and they're ready to change their savings portfolio. Individuals are doing this and seeing amazing results within their group. Individuals that were never able to save before are now saving money and their portfolio is growing steady. If you need more information about how to begin a group go to our website at: www.ephraimeconomics or www.drephraimincrease.wix.com/ephrai meconomics

Instant Savings

www.ingramcontent.com/pod-product-compliance
Lightning Source LLC
Chambersburg PA
CBHW060420190526
45169CB00002B/986